Beginning Consonant

Write the missing letter for each animal name.
Say the word.

1. __ear

2. __at

3. __og

4. __ish

5. __oat

6. __orse

7. __aguar

8. __angaroo

9. __ion

10. __ouse

11. __ightingale

12. __ig

13. __uail

14. __abbit

15. __eal

16. __iger

17. __ulture

18. __alrus

19. __ak

20. __ebra

1

Short Vowel Sounds: a

Read the short **a** words in the picture.
Then do what each sentence tells you.

at	as	cat
fan	am	ant
an	had	

1. Write the words that have two letters.

_____ _____ _____ _____

2. Write the words that have three letters.

_____ _____ _____ _____

Make short **a** words.
Write the short **a** endings.
Say the word.

at	**am**	**an**	**ad**
1. b ___	5. h ___	9. r ___	13. b ___
2. h ___	6. j ___	10. m ___	14. d ___
3. m ___	7. S ___	11. p ___	15. h ___
4. p ___	8. r ___	12. f ___	16. m ___

Short Vowel Sounds: e _____

Answer the riddles. Use the words in the box below.
Write the word on the line.

tent	**nest**	**bed**	**desk**
ten	**cent**	**belt**	**hen**
bell	**pen**	**red**	**sled**

1. We can ride on it in winter. _____

2. We write with it. _____

3. We can sleep in it outdoors. _____

4. It makes a ringing sound. _____

5. Firetrucks are often this color. _____

6. A dime is this many pennies. _____

7. It lays eggs. _____

8. We sit at one in school. _____

9. It holds up your pants. _____

10. We sleep on it. _____

11. A penny is one. _____

12. Baby birds stay in it. _____

Short Vowel Sounds: i

Write the short vowel **i** in the blanks to
complete the silly sentences.
Read the sentences to a friend.

1. I h __ d the l __ d, I d __ d.

2. I w __ ll f __ ll the h __ ll with flowers.

3. I w __ sh the f __ sh were still in the d __ sh.

4. The b __ g p __ g ate a f __ g.

Add the beginning letter to make short **i** words from the sentences above.

1. __ id	2. __ ill	3. __ ish	4. __ ig
__ id	__ ill	__ ish	__ ig
__ id	__ ill	__ ish	__ ig

Write two silly sentences with a short **i** word.

_____

_____

4

Short Vowel Sounds: o

Add an **o** to the letters to make short **o** words.

hot   **hop**   **rock**

1. n __ t   3. t __ p   5. s __ ck

2. p __ t   4. m __ p   6. l __ ck

Finish the sentence with a short **o** word.

got	top	job	doll
lot	box	hot	sock

1. Put the toys back in the _____ .

2. I cannot find my other _____ .

3. My sister _____ a bike for her birthday.

4. Be careful! The soup is _____ .

5. Zach's father has a new _____ .

6. There is snow on _____ of the mountain.

7. Mother made a new dress for my _____ .

8. There are a _____ of leaves to rake.

Short Vowel Sounds: u

Read the short **u** words in the umbrella.
Write two pairs of words that have the same ending.

1. _____   2. _____

_____   _____

bug
gum   cub
cup   bus   mug
fun   mud   sun

Write the beginning letter of each picture word
to make a word. The first one is done for you.

1. [pot] + [umbrella] + [pot]   p u p

2. [goat] + [umbrella] + [moon]   _ _ _

3. [gum] + [umbrella] + [nut]   _ _ _

4. [hat] + [umbrella] + [goat]   _ _ _

5. [ball] + [umbrella] + [goat]   _ _ _

6. [cat] + [umbrella] + [pot]   _ _ _

7. [scissors] + [umbrella] + [nut]   _ _ _

8. [moon] + [umbrella] + [dog]   _ _ _

6

REVIEW: Short Vowels

Add the correct short vowel to finish each word in the picture.
Each picture word has the same vowel sound.
Write the words on the lines under the correct vowel.

a

1. _____

_____

e

2. _____

_____

i

3. _____

_____

o

4. _____

_____

u

5. _____

_____

Long Vowel Sounds: a

The letters **ay** and **ai** make the long **a** sound.

Silly Snail is on the trail to get her pail.
What did she see on the way?
Write the name of each long **a** object
on the blanks. Use the words in the box.

jay	mail	train
tray	rain	paint
pail	hay	chain

Silent e

Add **e** to the word to make a long vowel word.
Then say the word.

1. can __   2. tub __   3. pin __   4. rob __   5. plan __

6. cub __   7. dim __   8. not __   9. rid __   10. sam __

11. cut __   12. cap __   13. kit __   14. tim __   15. tap __

Write the **bold** word from each sentence on the line.
Then add an **e**.
Read the sentence.

1. She **can** walk with a _____ .

2. The light was so **dim** I lost my _____ .

3. Dad did not **plan** to go by _____ .

4. I bought a **kit** to make a _____ .

5. **Sam** looks the _____ as he did last year.

Long Vowel Sounds: e

Long **e** sounds are made by **ea**, **ee**, or **ey**.

Write the words to finish the puzzle.

dream	bean	key
clean	leave	seed
money	tree	see

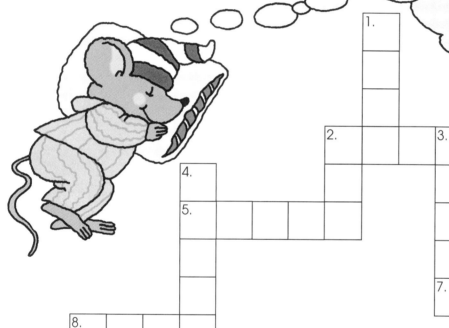

Across

2. produces a plant

5. go away

7. used to buy things

8. a kind of vegetable

Down

1. a large plant

2. look at

3. it happens when asleep

4. the opposite of dirty

6. opens locks

Long Vowel Sounds: i

The letters **y**, **igh** and sometimes **ie** have the long **i** sound.

Color the long **i** words red. Color the words that are not long **i** blue.

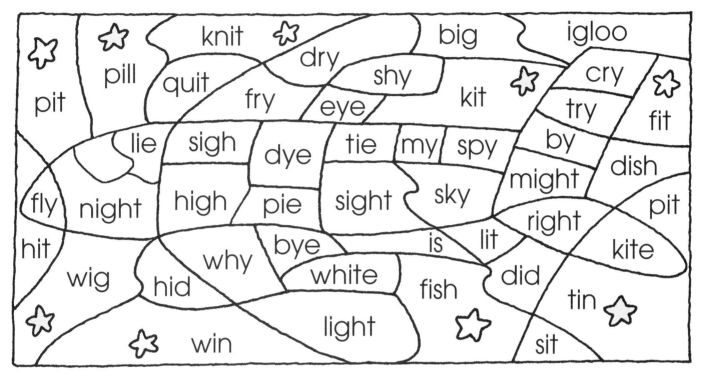

Write the long **i** words from above to complete the story.

It is **n** __ __ __ **t**. There is no **l** __ __ __ **t** in the **sk** __ . We heard a

plane **fl** __ **b** __ **h** __ __ __ above us. Seth let out a **s** __ __ __ .

"Someday," he said, "I will **tr** __ to learn how to **fl** __ .

But **r** __ __ __ **t** now, let's go have a piece of Mom's **p** __ __ !"

Long Vowel Sounds: o

The letters **oa** and **ow** usually make the long **o** sound.

Write the words to finish the puzzle.

snow	goat	toast	road
show	low	slow	grow

Across

2. another name for a movie

3. get bigger

4. browned bread

6. a highway

Down

1. opposite of high

2. frozen rain

3. a farm animal with horns

5. opposite of fast

Long Vowel Sounds: u _____

The letters **ew**, **u-e**, **ue**, and **ui** make the long **u** sound.

Use long **u** letter combinations to finish the words in each group.
Write the whole word on the line. Say the word.

ew

1. n ___   _____

2. d ___   _____

3. bl ___   _____

u-e

4. h __ g __   _____

5. c __ b __   _____

6. t __ b __   _____

ue

7. d ___   _____

8. gl ___   _____

9. bl ___   _____

ui

10. fr ___ t   _____

11. j ___ ce   _____

12. s ___ t   _____

REVIEW: Long Vowels

Write the words to finish the puzzle.

light	dime	honey	boat
new	rain	play	clean

Down

1. not heavy

3. food made by bees

5. free from dirt

8. never used

Across

2. equal to ten pennies

4. small ship

6. you do this to an instrument

7. drops of water from clouds

Blends: fl

This is Flora's first day of school.
Can you help Flora with her blends?

Use the **fl** words in the box to finish the puzzle.

flower	fly	floor
flame	flute	flag

Across

1. an insect

2. we stand on it

3. it can make music

Down

1. a rose is one

2. light given off from fire

3. all countries have one

Blends: pl, sl

It is time for recess on the playground.

Write the **sl** words on the slide.
Write the **pl** words on the plane.

planet	plane	plate
sleep	plant	slip
sled	slam	
please	slice	

Blends: bl, cl, gl

Help the class do a blend puzzle.

Read each clue. Use the words in the box to finish the puzzle.

blue	**clock**	**clean**	**glue**
blocks	**cloud**	**glad**	**glove**
black	**clothes**	**globe**	

Across
2. opposite of white
4. holds things together
5. a form of moisture in the sky
7. building toys
9. a round map
10. opposite of dirty

Down
1. what we wear
3. it keeps time
4. happy
6. worn on the hand
8. color of the sky

17

REVIEW: Blends

Today Glen came to our class. Learn more about Glen.

Underline the words that begin with the following blends.

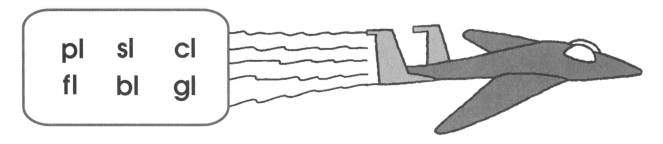

| pl | sl | cl |
| fl | bl | gl |

Glen is a pilot. His plane is silver and black. He flies

high in the clear, blue sky. Glen glides above the

clouds. He flies his plane around the globe. When

Glen sleeps, nobody knows.

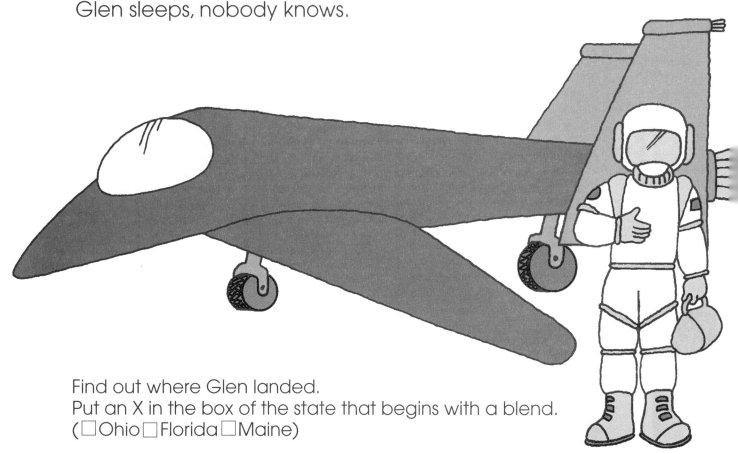

Find out where Glen landed.
Put an X in the box of the state that begins with a blend.
(☐ Ohio ☐ Florida ☐ Maine)

REVIEW: Blends

Common blends are: **bl**, **gl**, **cl**, **pl**, **fl**, and **sl**.

Write the **l** blends to make new words.
Say each word.
Find each blend word in the puzzle below.

1. **bl**

___ock

___ue

___ink

2. **gl**

___ad

___obe

___itter

3. **cl**

___own

___ock

___ub

4. **pl**

___an

___ay

___us

5. **fl**

___ower

___ag

___y

6. **sl**

___ip

___eep

___ow

```
B L I N K B L O C K G S G
P L U S S L I P L F L D L
C L U B W U R N O D A U O
N S K I C E N A W L D P B
F L A G S L O W N T S L E
L E O C P C L O C K E A G
Y E B G L I T T E R O Y T
T P L A N L F L O W E R F
```

Blends: br

Brent made a talking machine at school.
It makes **br** words.

Find the words the machine made.
Write the **br** words on the blanks.

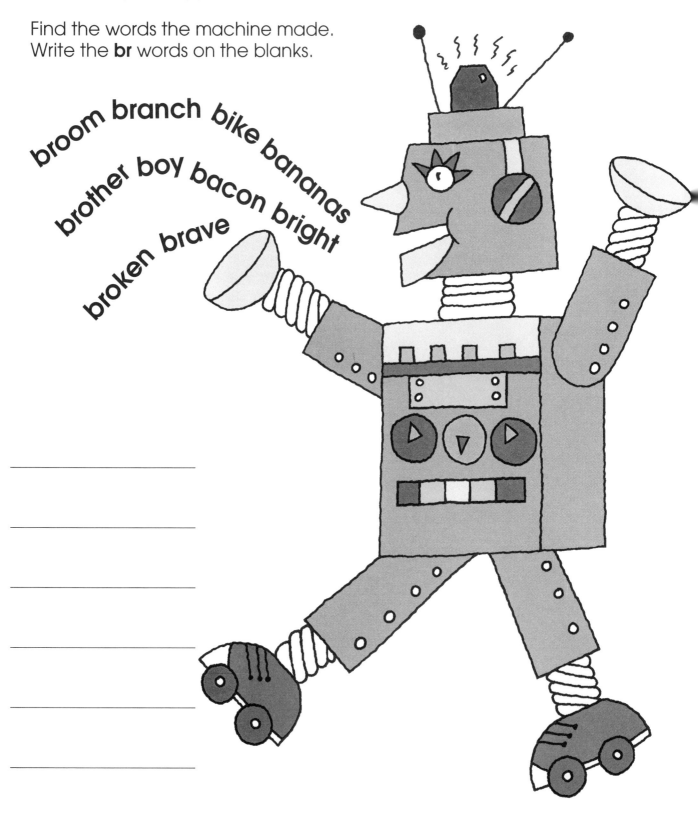

broom branch bike bananas
brother boy bacon bright
broken brave

_____

_____

_____

_____

_____

20

Blends: cr

Chris is in art class. He is coloring **cr** words.

Help Chris color the words red that begin with **cr**.

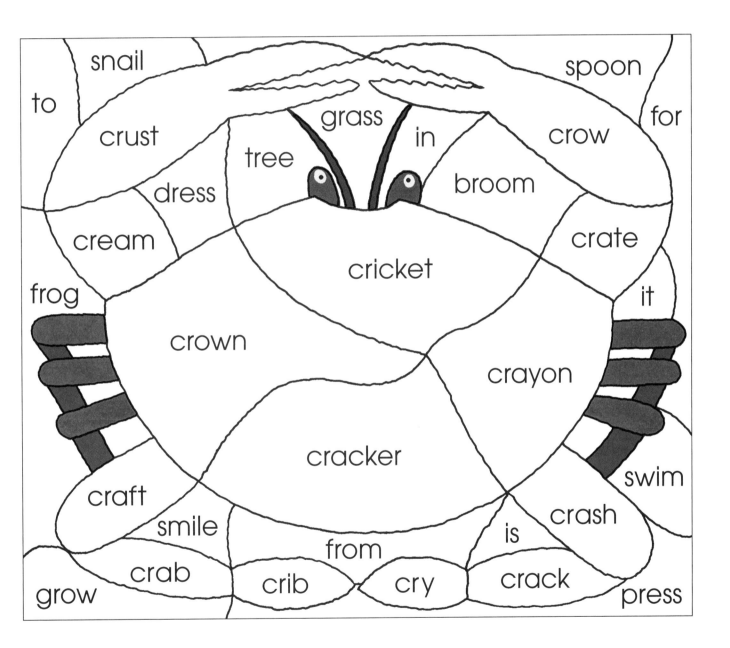

Chris colored a crazy _____ .

Blends: dr

Drinda has dreams of **dr** words.

Circle the words in her dream that begin with **dr**.

draw   drink   monkey

drum   lion   clock

nothing

mine   drip

dragon

driver

please   dress

dark   dry

zebra

Blends: fr

Fred is helping Frances learn **fr** words.

Write the correct **fr** word on the line to answer the riddle.

frog	front
from	fruit
friend	free

1. Someone you like is a _____.

2. It is not the back. It is the _____.

3. Maria got a present _____ Jimmy.

4. A _____ is a green animal that hops.

5. Bananas are a _____ and so are apples.

6. We rode every ride because the tickets were _____.

Blends: gr

Greg had to write a paper about himself.
What did Greg write?

Write the missing **gr** words on the correct lines.

group	grape	growl	grunt
grass	grow	green	Greg

My name is _____. I like to play outside on the

_____ _____. Sometimes I pretend to

be a monster, and I _____ and _____.

I play monster with a _____ of friends.

Then Mom makes peanut butter and _____ jelly

sandwiches for us. Even monsters need food to _____!

24

Blends: tr

Trina is trying to trick Trent.
She made a **tr** crossword.

Write the missing letters to make **tr** words.
Find each word within the puzzle.

_____ actor   _____ ee   _____ ick

_____ ain   _____ y   _____ ip

_____ uck   _____ ap   _____ ue

```
T R U C K T R Y
R R U E K T V R
A T R I P R T H
C R E C R I Y T
T R E E A C I R
O H T S A K P U
R U T R A P E E
P W T R A I N I
```

Blends: tr

Travis is in study hall. Help Travis with his homework.

Finish the puzzle with a rhyming word.

true   trap   truck
tree   trip   trick

Across

2. slip

3. luck

4. bee

Down

1. clap

2. stick

3. blue

Blends: pr

Priscilla has a birthday party today.
Find out what the class will give her.

Write the **pr** blend on the blanks to make words.
Then connect the dots.

1. __ __ **etty** •

2. __ __ **ess** •

3. __ __ **esent** •

• 6. __ __ **ize**

• 5. __ __ **ince**

• 4. __ __ **oud**

Priscilla's classmates will give her a _____ .

Blends: r

Color the **r** blends green to make a picture.
Choose a blend word to fill the blanks below.

br   **fr**   **pr**   **gr**   **dr**   **cr**   **tr**

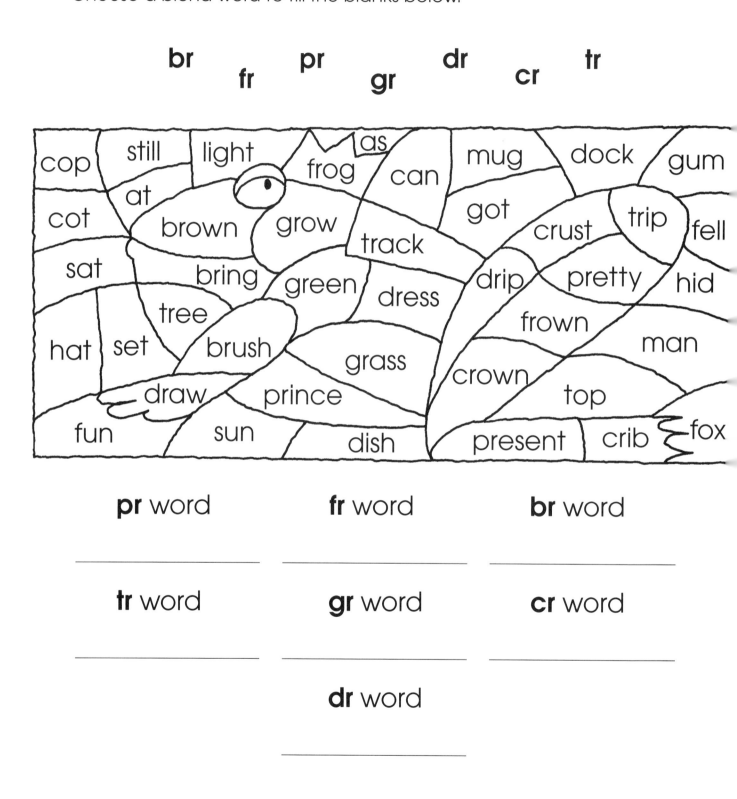

pr word   **fr** word   **br** word

_____   _____   _____

tr word   **gr** word   **cr** word

_____   _____   _____

dr word

_____

REVIEW: Blends

Make blend words by adding the **bold** ending.
Say each word.
The first one is done for you.

1. gr**ay**   M a y   tr___   pl___

2. cr**y**   fr__   fl__   sk__

3. dr**ip**   fl___   sl___   sk___

4. gr**ow**   bl___   cr___   sl___

5. br**own**   dr____   fr____   cl____

6. sk**ill**   sp____   st____   gr____

7. cr**ack**   tr____   bl____   st____

8. br**ing**   cl____   fl____   st____

REVIEW: Blends

It is Fun Day at recess. The students are on a treasure hunt.

Write the correct blend to finish each word. What will they find?

br   **cr**   **dr**   **fr**   **gr**   **pr**   **tr**

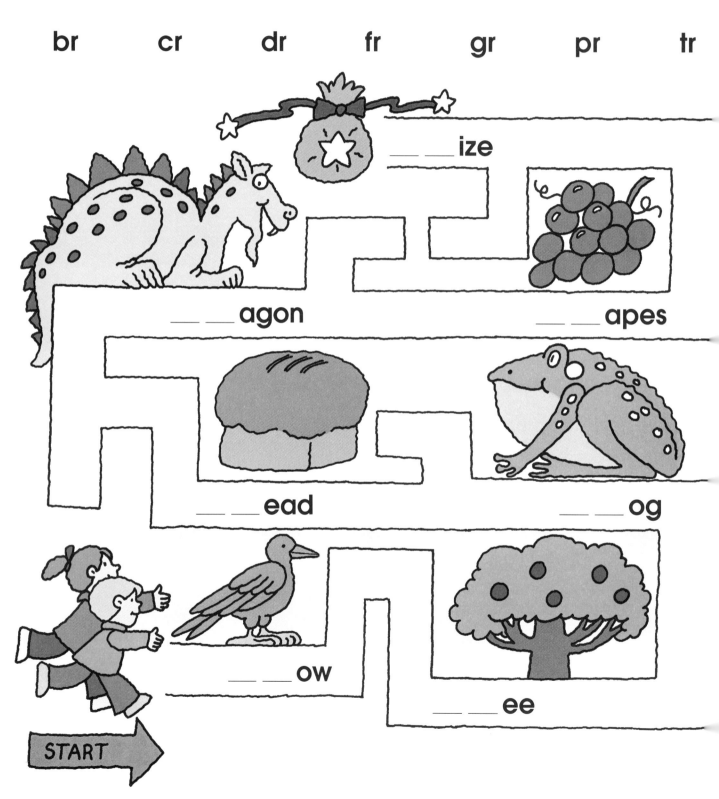

___ ___ **ize**

___ ___ **agon**

___ ___ **apes**

___ ___ **ead**

___ ___ **og**

___ ___ **ow**

___ ___ **ee**

START

Blends: sm, sn

Sam's snail is on his way to school.
Help Sam follow his trail.

Write the **sm** or **sn** blend to finish the word.

___ ___owman

___ ___oke

___ ___ake

___ ___ell

___ ___og

___ ___ile

___ ___art

___ ___ail

The class is taking a trip. Help them find the zoo.

Draw a line to connect all the **st** words.
The words may begin or end with **st**.

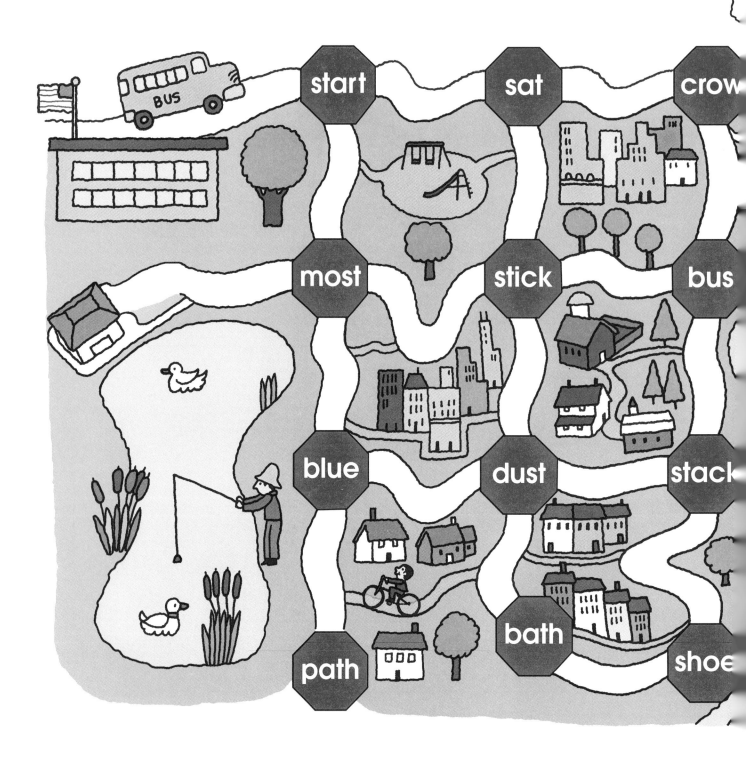

Blends: sw, sp

Swain and Spencer are at a swim meet.
Help them stay in their lanes.

Write the **sw** or **sp** blend to finish the word.

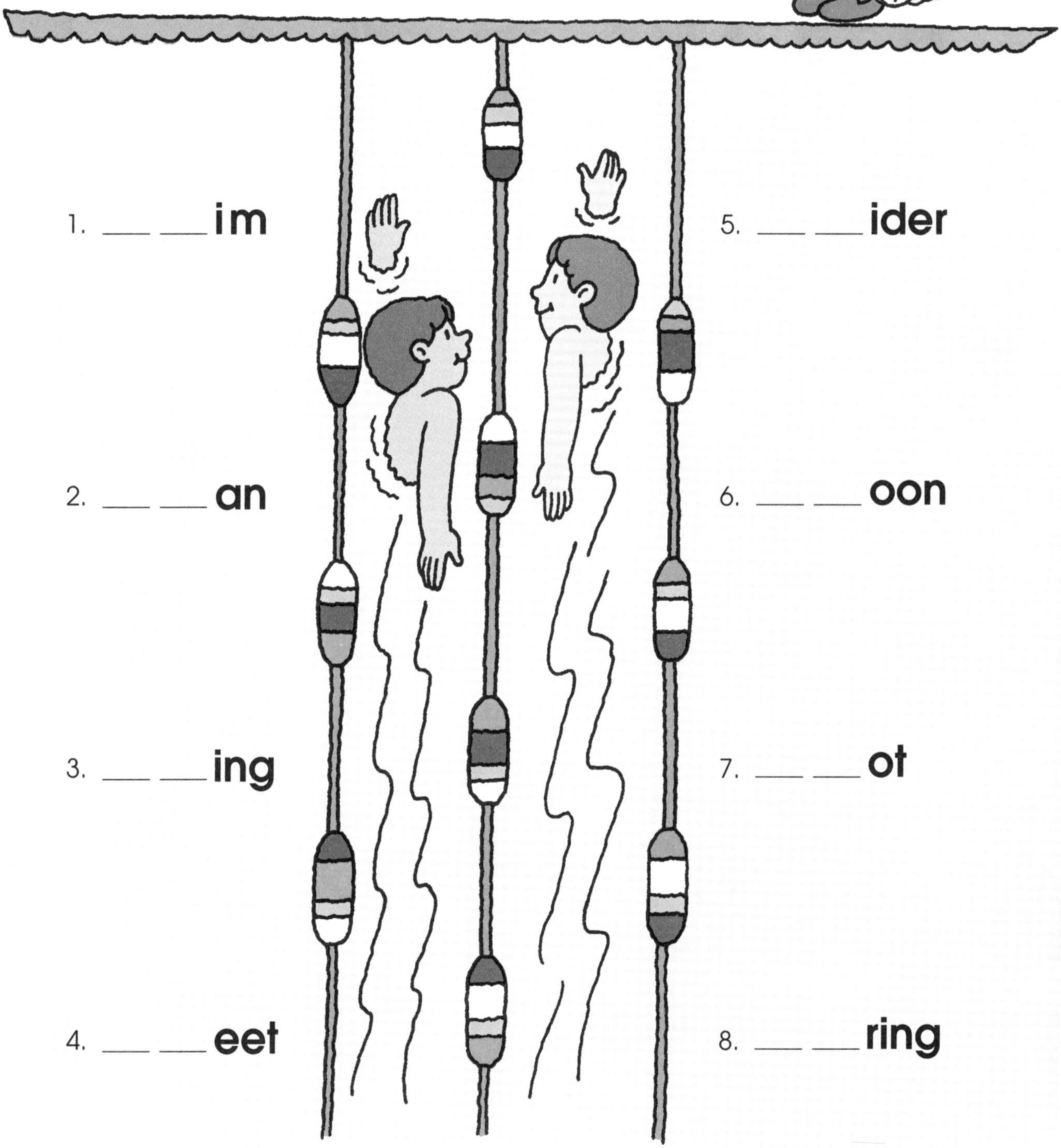

1. __ __ **im**

2. __ __ **an**

3. __ __ **ing**

4. __ __ **eet**

5. __ __ **ider**

6. __ __ **oon**

7. __ __ **ot**

8. __ __ **ring**

Blends: str, spr

It is show and tell time at school. What will Jill tell?

Write the correct **str** or **spr** words on the lines to finish the story.

| street | strawberry | spray |
| stream | sprinkler | spring |

Dad had to water the new _____

plants. He put the _____ by the plants.

Then he turned on the water. A big _____ of water

shot into the air. It began to make a long _____

down the _____. Dad had to fix a bad

_____. Now we have lots of juicy berries to share.

Blends: s

Write the **s** blends to make new words. Say each word.
Complete the story below with **s** blend words.

1. **sk** __ __ in

__ __ ip

2. **sh** __ __ ape

__ __ ell

3. **sp** __ __ eed

__ __ ill

4. **st** __ __ ory

__ __ amp

5. **sl** __ __ eep

__ __ ime

6. **sn** __ __ ap

__ __ ail

7. **sm** __ __ oke

__ __ all

8. **sw** __ __ eet

__ __ im

This is a **st** __ __ __ of a **sm** __ __ __ **sn** __ __ __ named **Sk** __ __.

Sk __ __ lives in a curly **sh** __ __ __. His **sk** __ __ feels

like **sl** __ __ __. **Sp** __ __ __ does not matter to him. If he is in

danger, he goes into his **sh** __ __ __. He also goes into his

sh __ __ __ to **sl** __ __ __. **Sw** __ __ __ dreams, **Sk** __ __!

REVIEW: Blends

Take a test with the class. Look at the picture. Say the word.
Circle the correct blend. Write the blend on the blanks.

Name: _____

1. **str**   **sl**

   __ __ __ **awberry**

2. **sl**   **sn**

   __ __ **ail**

3. **sm**   **st**

   __ __ **amp**

4. **spr**   **str**

   __ __ __ **inkler**

5. **str**   **sw**

   __ __ __ **eam**

6. **sl**   **sm**

   __ __ **ile**

7. **sw**   **st**

   __ __ **im**

8. **sl**   **st**

   __ __ **ar**

REVIEW: Blends

Clara forgot to finish the blend words.

Write the missing letters to make a word.

ue	ee	ib	ock	ink
ag	og	ot	ove	owman

1. **bl** __ __

2. **fr** __ __

3. **sp** __ __

4. **tr** __ __

5. **gl** __ __ __

6. **fl** __ __

7. **cl** __ __ __

8. **cr** __ __

9. **dr** __ __ __

10. **sn** __ __ __ __ __

38

REVIEW: Blends

The children have their mittens mixed up.

Draw lines to show which mittens go together.

Say the words.

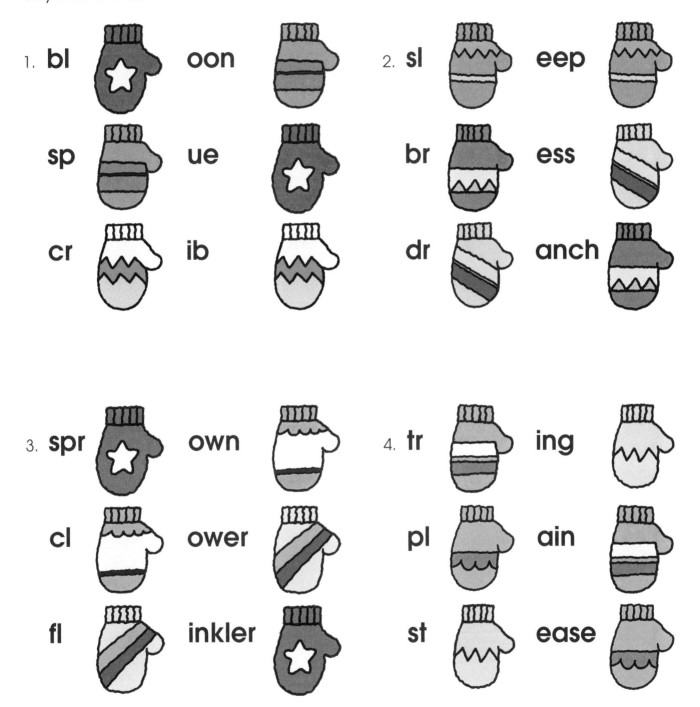

1. bl   oon

   sp   ue

   cr   ib

2. sl   eep

   br   ess

   dr   anch

3. spr   own

   cl   ower

   fl   inkler

4. tr   ing

   pl   ain

   st   ease

REVIEW: Blends

Brent has homework to do.
Help Brent finish the puzzle.

Jack	click	brown
crack	black	clown

Across

2. opposite of white

3. a funny person

4. a break

Down

1. a name

2. a color

3. a sound

Combination Sounds: ch ————

Chad and Mitch have a **ch** project.
They need objects with the **ch** sound.

Draw a line from each word that **starts** with **ch** to Chad.
Draw a line from each word that **ends** with **ch** to Mitch.

cheese

porch

cow

dog

chair

banana

smile

watch

fish

bird

chimney

bear

catch

match

book

glass

cherry

man

Combination Sounds: th

Help Thelma and Meredith write a paper.

Finish each sentence with the correct **th** word.

bath	**path**
there	**Thank**
thirty	**think**

Our dog, Rex, would not let us give him a _____.

We _____ he's afraid of water. Rex tried to run from us, but

we followed his _____. It took us almost _____

minutes to catch him. _____ goodness Mom was

_____ to help us!

42

Combination Sounds: sh _____

The class took a **sh** field trip.
They went to a sheep farm and a fish farm.

Write all the words that start with **sh** in the sheep pen.
Write all the words that end in **sh** in the fish pond.

push	**shop**	**shoe**
show	**dish**	**shirt**
shell	**wash**	**wish**

1. _____

2. _____

3. _____

4. _____

5. _____

6. _____

7. _____

8. _____

9. _____

Combination Sounds: wh

Mrs. White wants the class to learn how to whistle.
Help them whistle to all the **wh** words.

Write the missing letters to make **wh** words.
Find each word within the puzzle.

___ eel ___ y ___ en

___ eat ___ ale ___ at

___ istle ___ ite ___ ere

```
W H I S T L E
H H A W H Y W
A R W H A T H
L N X I T W E
E W H T T H R
W H E E L E E
W H E A T N S
```

REVIEW: Combination Sounds

Some letters make a new sound when they are put together.

> **shell**   **cherry**   **third**   **think**
> **wheel**   **whale**   **ship**   **chair**

Write the words from the box above that **begin** like the following words.

1. **ch**ild   _____   _____

2. **th**ick   _____   _____

3. **wh**ite   _____   _____

4. **sh**op   _____   _____

> **north**   **watch**   **fish**

Write the words from the box above that **end** like the following words.

5. ea**ch**   _____

6. ba**th**   _____

7. wa**sh**   _____

REVIEW: Blends

It is time for lunch. What is on the menu?

Write the missing letters on the blanks.

ch   th
sh   wh

__ __ite milk

__ __eat bread

__ __icken sandwi__ __

bro __ __

__ __erry pie

Soft __ __ell tacos

REVIEW: Blends

It is summer vacation. Keep your skills sharp.

Write the missing letters to make words that end with **ch**, **sh**, and **th** sounds. Then find each word in the puzzle.

mat___   wa___   mou___

chur___   pu___   sou___

wat___   di___   pa___

por___   ba___

W P A T H W D M
B O H S J A I O
A R I O K T S U
T C H U R C H T
H H M T T H L H
P U S H W A S H
M A T C H W E L

REVIEW: Blends

School is over for the year.
What does Shelly find in her desk?

Draw a line from each picture to the
sound you hear in each word.

ch   sh   th   wh

REVIEW: Blends

Help the class learn about snails.

Underline each word that begins with the sounds in the box.

sn	sl	cr	pl
st	sh	gr	

A snail has a soft body covered by a shell. It creeps along on a
foot. Its body has a head with feelers, eyes, a mouth, and tiny
teeth. Land snails live in shady places. They lay eggs in the
ground. A moving snail makes a sticky slime to help it move.
Snails live almost everywhere.

Same Sounds: oi, oy

The letters **oi** and **oy** have the same sound.

Find each word in the puzzle below.

boil	joy	point	broil
oil	toy	soil	moist
join	boy	coin	voice

```
B N S O I L L C O R T
R T U E S J O Y L F O
O L N B P E I N B O Y
I L A B O I L K N T S
L S V R I S T J W L F
L E O C N L C O I N O
M O I S T I U I E R I
T P C A N L F N O W S
W E E O K T P G A V E
```

Write a sentence using an **oi** word.

_____

Write a sentence using an **oy** word.

_____

Letter Combinations: oo, ue, ew

Answer the riddles. Use the words in the box below.
Write the word on the line.

moose	**blue**	**tooth**	**pool**
school	**true**	**stool**	**dew**
broom	**glue**	**chew**	**new**

1. It is the color of the sky. _____

2. You can find this on the grass in the morning. _____

3. Things stick together with it. _____

4. It is a big animal with antlers. _____

5. It is the opposite of old. _____

6. This is what you do with gum. _____

7. You can sit on it. _____

8. You can sweep the floor with it. _____

9. It is the opposite of false. _____

10. You should brush it twice a day. _____

11. This is where you go to learn. _____

12. You go swimming in this. _____

Letter Combinations: ou, ow

Answer the riddles. Use the words in the box below.
Write the word on the line.

brown	**crown**	**sour**
hound	**mouse**	**out**
clown	**howl**	

1. A lemon is this. _____

2. Tree trunks are this color. _____

3. A king wears one. _____

4. This word means the opposite of in. _____

5. A hunting dog is sometimes called this. _____

6. This is a funny person in a circus. _____

7. Wolves make this sound. _____

8. It is a rodent with small ears and a long tail. _____

Write two sentences. Use an **ow** word in one sentence
and an **ou** word in the other.

_____

_____

52

Silent Letters

Sometimes the letters **l**, **k**, **w**, **h**, **t**, **b**, and **gh** are silent.

Add the silent letters.
Then say the word.

1. **w**

_ rap

_ rong

_ rite

2. **gh**

hi _ _

si _ _

ni _ _ t

3. **b**

dum _

thum _

crum _

4. **t**

ca _ ch

ma _ ch

swi _ ch

5. **k**

_ nob

_ nit

_ nee

6. **l**

wa _ k

sta _ k

ta _ k

7. **h**

_ onest

_ our

g _ ost

See if you can finish each word.

8. ri _ _ t

9. lam _

10. ca _ f

11. _ rite

12. la _ ch

13. _ nock

14. _ onor

15. bri _ _ t

16. ki _ chen

Same Sounds: ir, er, ur

The letter combinations **ir**, **er**, and **ur** have the same **r** sound.

Write the words to finish the puzzle.

farmer	bird	purse
father	girl	shirt
dinner	nurse	turtle

Across

2. a person who works on a farm

5. a sister is one

6. a feathered animal

7. a cloth garment with collar and sleeves

8. used to carry money and small objects

Down

1. a person who cares for the sick

2. the male parent

3. one of three daily meals

4. a reptile with a shell

54

Different Sounds: c, g

Copy the words. Say each word.

The letter **c** sounds like **k** before these vowels: **a o u**.

1. cat _____

2. cow _____

3. cake _____

4. cup _____

The letter **c** sounds like **s** before these vowels: **i e y**.

5. city _____

6. circus _____

7. cent _____

8. cycle _____

The letter **g** sounds like **g** in goat before these vowels: **a o u**.

9. gas _____

10. gum _____

11. good _____

12. got _____

The letter **g** usually sounds like **j** before these vowels: **i e y**.

13. gym _____

14. gem _____

15. gentle _____

16. giraffe _____

Contractions

When you use an apostrophe to put words together, you form a contraction.

Choose the correct contraction to finish the sentence.

aren't	I'll	they'll
don't	isn't	they're
can't	We're	couldn't

1. The socks _____ match.
   do not

2. I _____ read her writing.
   could not

3. _____ going on vacation tomorrow.
   We are

4. Hanna _____ home.
   is not

5. _____ bake cookies tonight.
   I will

6. Why _____ the dogs in the pen?
   are not

7. I was told _____ on the way home.
   they are

8. Seth _____ find his baseball.
   cannot

9. Our grandparents said _____ see us Saturday.
   they will

56

Compound Words

Make one word out of two!

Look at the pictures.
Then write the compound word on the line.
The first one is done for you.

1. _football_

2. _____

3. _____

4. _____

5. _____

6. _____

7. _____

Plural Endings

Plural means more than one. Here are some different ways to make a word plural. Sometimes you add **s**. Write the word, adding **s**.

1. book _____
2. hand _____
3. doll _____
4. clock _____
5. flower _____
6. mother _____

When the word ends in **x**, **ss**, **ch**, or **sh**, you add **es**.

7. box _____
8. dress _____
9. wish _____
10. pitch _____
11. bench _____
12. dish _____

When the word ends in **y**, usually you change the **y** to **i** and add **es**.

13. baby _____
14. pony _____
15. city _____
16. cherry _____
17. berry _____
18. penny _____

When the word ends in **f**, you change the **f** to **v** and add **es**.

19. leaf _____
20. wife _____
21. knife _____
22. shelf _____

58

Suffixes

Words can have different endings.

Read the directions for each group.
Write the word with the correct ending.
Say the word.

Add ing

1. think _____
2. sing _____
3. work _____

Add ness or less

4. sick _____
5. care _____
6. kind _____
7. help _____

Drop e and add ing

8. save _____
9. make _____
10. come _____

Double the last letter and add ing

11. run _____
12. swim _____
13. jog _____

Add er or est

14. fast _____
15. slow _____
16. old _____
17. hard _____

Add ful

18. care _____
19. thank _____
20. help _____

Prefixes: un, mis

Un in front of a word means **not**.
Finish the word puzzle using the prefix **un**.

1. not happy

u	n	h	a	p	p	y

2. not able

3. not safe

4. not kind

5. not even

6. not tied

Mis in front of a word means **wrong**.
Finish the word puzzle using the prefix **mis**.

7. wrong fit

8. wrong place

9. wrong deal

10. wrong fire

11. wrong count

12. wrong spell

60

Answer Key

Page 1
1. bear
2. cat
3. dog
4. fish
5. goat
6. horse
7. jaguar
8. kangaroo
9. lion
10. mouse
11. nightingale
12. pig
13. quail
14. rabbit
15. seal
16. tiger
17. vulture
18. walrus
19. yak
20. zebra

Page 2
1. at, an, am, as
2. cat, ant, had, fan

1. bat
2. hat
3. mat
4. pat
5. ham
6. jam
7. Sam
8. ram
9. ran
10. man
11. pan
12. fan
13. bad
14. dad
15. had
16. mad

Page 3
1. sled
2. pen
3. tent
4. bell
5. red
6. ten
7. hen
8. desk
9. belt
10. bed
11. cent
12. nest

Page 4
1. hid, lid, did
2. will, fill, hill
3. wish, fish, dish
4. big, pig, fig

Page 5
1. not
2. pot
3. top
4. mop
5. sock
6. lock

1. box
2. sock
3. got
4. hot
5. job
6. top
7. doll
8. lot

Page 6
1. bug/mug
2. sun/fun

1. **pup**
2. gum
3. fun
4. hug
5. bug
6. cup
7. sun
8. mud

Page 7
1. cat
   man
2. hen
   red
3. pig
   big
4. top
   hop
5. sun
   bus

Page 8
paint, chain, hay, rain, train, mail, tray, jay, pail

Page 9
1. cane
2. tube
3. pine
4. robe
5. plane
6. cube
7. dime
8. note
9. ride
10. same
11. cute
12. cape
13. kite
14. time
15. tape

1. cane
2. dime
3. plane
4. kite
5. same

Page 10
Crossword:
- t r e e (down)
- ²s e e d
- d r e a m
- ³c l e a v e
- ⁴e a / m o n e y
- k e y
- ⁵m e a n

Page 11
night, light, sky
fly, by, high, sigh
try, fly
right, pie

Page 12
Crossword:
- l o
- ²s h o w
- n o
- g r o w
- o a
- ⁴t o a s t
- l
- ⁵r o a d
- w

Page 13
1. new
2. dew
3. blew
4. huge
5. cube
6. tube

7. due
8. glue
9. blue
10. fruit
11. juice
12. suit

Page 14
Crossword:
- l
- ¹d i m e
- g h
- ²h t
- ³b o a t
- n e
- ⁴c y
- p l a y
- ⁵r a i n
- n e
- w

Page 15

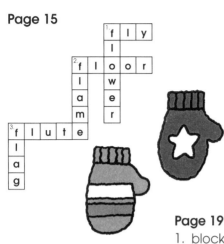

```
      ¹f l y
       l
   ²f l o o r
       a w
       m e
       r
  ³f l u t e
   l
   a
   g
```

Page 16

pl words:
plant, planet, plate, please, plane

sl words:
sleep, sled, slice, slam, slip

Page 17

```
           ¹c
   ²b l a c k    ⁴g l u e
      l o        l
      o t        a
      c h   ⁵c l o u d
   ⁶g  k e       k
   ⁷b l o c k s
      o v
   ⁸b u
  ⁹g l o b e
      u
 ¹⁰c l e a n
```

Page 18

Glen, plane, black, flies, clear, blue, Glen, glides, clouds, flies, plane, globe, Glen, sleeps
(Florida)

Page 19

1. block
   blue
   blink
2. glad
   globe
   glitter
3. clown
   clock
   club
4. plan
   play
   plus
5. flower
   flag
   fly
6. slip
   sleep
   slow

```
B L I N K B L O C K G S G
P L U S S L I P L F L D L
C L U B W U R N O A U O B
N S K I C E N A W L D P E
F L A G S L O W N T S L A
L E O C P C L O C K E A G
Y E B G L I T T E R O Y T
T P L A N L F L O W E R F
```

Page 20

brother, broom, broken, bright, brave, branch

Page 21

crust, cream, crown, cricket, cracker, crayon, crate, crow, craft, crab, crib, cry, crack, crash
(crab)

Page 22

draw, drink, drum, dragon, dress, drip, dry, driver

Page 23

1. friend
2. front
3. from
4. frog
5. fruit
6. free

Page 24

Greg, green, grass, grunt, growl, group, grape, grow

Page 25

```
T R U C K T R Y
R U E K T V R
A T R I P R T H
C R E C R I Y T
T R E E A C I R
O H T S A K P U
R U T R A P E E
P W T R A I N I
```

Page 26

```
        ¹t
         r
         a
     ²t r i p
         r
         i
         c
   ³t r u c k
       r
       u
  ⁴t r e e
```

Page 27

1. pretty
2. press
3. present
6. prize
5. prince
4. proud
(present)

Page 28

Automatic fill-in.

Page 29

1. tray, play
2. fry, fly, sky
3. flip, slip, skip
4. blow, crow, slow
5. drown, frown, clown
6. spill, still, grill
7. track, black, stack
8. cling, fling, sting

Page 30

prize, grapes, dragon, bread, frog, crow, tree

Page 31

snowman, smoke, snake, smell, smog, smile, smart, snail

Page 32-33

start, most, stick, dust, stack, just, stir, store, best, last

Page 34

1. swim	5. spider
2. swan	6. spoon
3. swing	7. spot
4. sweet	8. spin

Page 35

strawberry, sprinkler, spray, stream, street, spring

Page 36

1. skin	2. speed	3. story
skip	spill	stamp
4. sleep	5. snap	6. smoke
slime	snail	small
7. sweet		
swim		

story, small, snail, Skip
Skip, skin
slime, speed
sleep, sweet, Skip

Page 37

1. strawberry	2. snail
3. stamp	4. sprinkler
5. stream	6. smile
7. swim	8. star

Page 38

Accept answers that form words.

Page 39

1. blue	2. sleep
spoon	branch
crib	dress
3. sprinkler	4. train
clown	please
flower	sting

Page 40

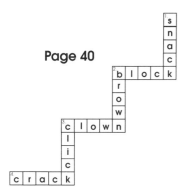

Page 41

Chad
chimney, cheese, cherry, chair

Mitch
porch, watch, match, catch

Page 42

bath, think, path, thirty, Thank, there

Page 43

1. shell	6. dish
2. show	7. push
3. shoe	8. wish
4. shirt	9. wash
5. shop	

Page 44

Page 45

1. cherry, chair
2. third, think
3. whale, wheel
4. shell, ship
5. watch
6. north
7. fish

Page 46

white milk
wheat bread
chicken sandwich
broth
cherry pie
soft shell tacos

Answer Key

Page 47

Page 48

ch
cherries, cheese, watch

sh
shirt, sheep, dish, shoe

th
bath, three

wh
whale, wheel, whistle

Page 49

snail, shell, creeps, snails, shady, places, ground, snail, sticky, slime, Snails

Page 51

1. blue	7. stool
2. dew	8. broom
3. glue	9. true
4. moose	10. tooth
5. new	11. school
6. chew	12. pool

Page 50

Page 52

1. sour
2. brown
3. crown
4. out
5. hound
6. clown
7. howl
8. mouse

Page 53

1. wrap wrong write	2. high sigh night	3. dumb thumb crumb	4. catch match switch
5. knob knit knee	6. walk stalk talk	7. honest hour ghost	

8. right   11. write   14. honor
9. lamb   12. latch   15. bright
10. calf   13. knock   16. kitchen

Page 54

(crossword)
farmer, girl, d, a, g, n, t, i, n, h, n, nurse, e, e, bird, shirt, t, purse, se, u, r, t, l, e

Page 55

1. cat	5. city	9. gas	13. gym
2. cow	6. circus	10. gum	14. gem
3. cake	7. cent	11. good	15. gentle
4. cup	8. cycle	12. got	16. giraffe

Page 56

1. don't
2. couldn't
3. We're
4. isn't
5. I'll
6. aren't
7. they're
8. can't
9. they'll

Page 57

2. birdhouse
3. rainbow
4. doorbell
5. starfish
6. watchdog
7. fireman

Page 58

1. books	4. clocks
2. hands	5. flowers
3. dolls	6. mothers
7. boxes	10. pitches
8. dresses	11. benches
9. wishes	12. dishes
13. babies	16. cherries
14. ponies	17. berries
15. cities	18. pennies
19. leaves	21. knives
20. wives	22. shelves

Page 59

1. thinking	11. running
2. singing	12. swimming
3. working	13. jogging
4. sickness	14. faster, fastest
5. careless	15. slower, slowest
6. kindness	16. older, oldest
7. helpless	17. harder, hardest
8. saving	18. careful
9. making	19. thankful
10. coming	20. helpful

Page 60

2. unable	7. misfit
3. unsafe	8. misplace
4. unkind	9. misdeal
5. uneven	10. misfire
6. untied	11. miscount
	12. misspell